How to Love a Good Woman:
on a Shoestring Budget

How to Love a Good Woman:
on a Shoestring Budget

JAVIER

Writers Club Press
San Jose New York Lincoln Shanghai

How to Love a Good Woman: on a Shoestring Budget

Writers Club Press
an imprint of iUniverse, Inc.

For information address:
iUniverse, Inc.
5220 S. 16th St., Suite 200
Lincoln, NE 68512
www.iuniverse.com

ISBN: 0-595-21087-2

Printed in the United States of America

To My Wife
T. L. Thompson
To Whom I Pledge My Allegiance And Love

GOD SAVE MY QUEEN

"NEXT TO GOD WE ARE INDEBTED TO WOMEN, FIRST FOR LIFE ITSELF, AND THEN FOR MAKING IT WORTH LIVING."

—MARY MCLEOD BETHUNE

ACKNOWLEDGEMENTS

To my Lord and Savior, Jesus Christ, for being Love. To my wife, Tesha, who is perfect for me but accepts me with all my faults and allows me to practice my love. Romance without love is dead. To my mother, Dorothy Thompson, who taught me how to love by loving me. To my father, Beverette Thompson, who taught me that it's O.K. for a man to love out loud.

To my friend and mentor, Jerome Foster, who encourages me by example. Thank you for showing a personal interest in me. In all I do I'm determined to never let you down.

I would like to personally thank everyone who helped me finish this book, but that would fill a book of it's own. Thankfully, those people know who they are.

CONTENTS

IN LOVING MEMORY
OF
JOANNA THOMPSON

Ariana is your true reflection. I can hardly wait until she's talking to see if her voice matches my memories of yours.

Sleep Peacefully

INTRODUCTION

First of all, I want it to be understood that I am writing this book against my will. My wife has literally forced my hands to the keyboard and threatened to cut off my love support until the first copy is sold. I, on the other hand, would like nothing more than to finish my hot chocolate and crawl back into bed.

Honestly, the very act of writing this book goes against everything we are taught in the underground men's movement. But since I am being forced at love point, let's get started.

If some of the things I say come off as a little "male chauvinistic", it's because I am. No, I do not believe that women are by any means less than men are. It just means that I believe in "roles". Admitting this helps me understand my role as "servant". My dad was a servant. His dad was a servant. I come from a long line of proud servants. By the time you finish this book I hope you too can proudly look into the mirror and declare yourself a "servant" to your loved one.

If you find it hard to say that you are a servant, that's your first clue that you might be with the wrong person. Those of you who have found that magical person you love and adore understand what I'm talking about. Those of you, who are in a relationship with someone "crazy", close your textbooks for a moment and read over our shoulders. Better yet, read over my shoulder. Let me tell you about my wife, Tesha.

I really do believe the sun rises and sets with Tesha. She takes complete care of me. This woman cooks for me; cleans up after my three tornado offspring and me; irons our clothes; licks our wounds and makes love so good she could make a homeless man build a house. I have been making love to this woman for close to a decade now and every time we do I just want to call my momma! When I greet her parents, I spend thirty minutes hugging them and until they read this book they had no idea why. Now that is good loving and the reason why I'm proud to wear the name servant! I am in charge of anything it takes to make that woman smile. That's my role. That's my job.

Those of you who don't understand this kind of love and devotion because you are connected somehow to a "crazy" person may now go back to your own textbooks.

Now, before we go on, I feel I must clarify this word, "crazy". "Crazy", is someone who does not fully understand his or her "role". Remember that word? If a woman understood her "role" she would quickly make you into a happy servant so that you could please her more. Any woman who does not want to be pleased more is simply "crazy".

My mother said, "People just don't wake up crazy". That means either you were not paying attention or chose to look over this little human flaw when you first saw it. Whatever the case, you are now in a world of pain and you have my sympathy. It's very hard to free yourself of a crazy person. If you've been with this crazy person for a length of time, most likely some of the "crazy" has rubbed off on you. On the other hand, if your relationship is not going well and you have tried all the techniques I will give you in this book, you may need to seek at least thirty minutes a week on somebody's couch. Hopefully this person will have a psychiatric degree from a fully accredited university and not be too expensive. Just tell them that you have discovered the crazy person in your relationship and it isn't your spouse.

WARNING: This is not a quick fix diet. The changes we make will have to become life changes. We have all heard that whatever it took to get her it takes to keep her. Tesha knows she is second only to God! Not a second should pass away that your lady does not feel this way. Are you a work-aholic? There's nothing wrong with that if you are both enjoying the fruits of your labor. If you are not, then for what are you working so hard? I can hear you whispering in the back of your head, "I work hard to guarantee our future", and you are right. I guarantee that if there are kids involved alimony and child support will be very expensive!

How To Use This Book

This book should be used to get your romantic juices flowing. I'll give you a couple of things that I have found but don't copy them exactly. Mold them into your lifestyle. I know what my lady likes because I listen but I don't have to tell you that women are different. What I will tell you is that I have tested this book on different women from different walks of life and the reactions seem to be the same: "Thank you, Jesus! Finally someone knows what we want!" A lady in Denver, Colorado told me that she was going to place this book on her coffee table and use it for a prerequisite for dating.

So how did you come across this book? Was it given to you or did you buy it? If you bought it, good for you! It means you are actively trying to improve your love life. If this book was given to you, well, let's just get started.

Read this book with a pen or pencil in hand. In some sections you will be asked to express yourself. Just write your answers in the space provided. After most sections you will find a page or two for notes. Maybe something you read inspired you to create a personal romantic idea of your own. Don't wait! Write it down before you forget! When you finish the book read it again. You may find that your answers changed as you got the full romantic picture. This book should become personal to you. Hopefully, if you took good notes, it should seem as if we both wrote it. I'll provide the clues and you solve your own romance mystery.

Here is your first clue:

(Paying attention + The desire to totally please your lady) x Creativity = Romance

Write that equation down. It will help you solve any romantic problem you should ever come up against. There will be a quiz at the end but the person who bought this book for you will give it. My advice to you is don't fail it!

The Budget

Hey, how do you like that title? A budget does not mean that you are finding a creative way to be cheap! It means that you don't have a lot of money at this point in your life so you must find another way to show the love of your life how much you adore her. It's not that we are cheap. It's just that we are broke! But you know what my mother says? "If she's there with you in the rough years, she'll be there with you in the good years". Well, Tesha and I have always been broke but we have always had good years. As a matter of fact, our brokest years where our best by far! I remember when all we had to eat for a week was chicken and noodles. We went from "Chicken Surprise" on Monday to "Chicken, You Know It" on Friday. But we were happy.

We joked about our misfortune and it helped us laugh instead of cry. I lay awake in my bed sometimes and think about how hard those days could have been if I was with someone "crazy". Laughter in a relationship is so important. You have to be able to really enjoy each other. Turn off the TV tonight and see if you and your mate really have anything in common. Ask her about her goals in life. Then listen. If you feel adventurous, ask her what would make you a better lover. Then listen. If you find yourself sitting on the couch staring at the wall, you might have some thinking to do. One of you may be crazy!

Don't be surprised that in planning your budget you figure out that this person is not the one for you. One couple in particular comes to mind. They are married now and all they seem to do is fuss and complain about little things. It's as if they never "dated" at all. You remember dating right? It's that period of time before marriage when you are supposed to figure out if this person is truly a good match for you. With that in mind, let's plan and budget a special night. And remember, we are on a "shoestring" budget because rent is due and we are still working on our financial goals.

Our budget will be $30. For those of you who don't have $30, I suggest you start a newspaper route with your spare time! If you can't find $30 to spend on someone you plan on spending the rest of your life with that could be a huge clue to who's "crazy" in your relationship.

Our new word for today is "SURPRISE"! Mrs. Dorothy Thompson, my mother, said women love surprises!

Pick a room of the apartment, your home, the basement; it doesn't matter just so you two will be alone. Now, remove anything that kills the mood; couch, TV, boxes. Let's focus our attention to the center of the room. We'll need a small table with two chairs as nice as you can "borrow". Drape it with a white bed sheet even if you own a tablecloth. A sheet will fall around the legs to give it a nice romantic look.

Assuming we have nothing, let's take a trip to the store.
Any "Dollar Store" will do. First we pick up the centerpiece for the table; the candle. We will also need scotch tape, two or three different colors of gift ribbon and two packs of balloons.

It may be obvious now that we are preparing dinner so let's get that out of the way. Tonight we are having pizza! Yes, pizza! And guess what? You're both getting dressed for it! We are going to order it and here is the catch, go pick it up. It's much cheaper. Plus, she will never know it! The food will not be late and by picking it up you save money and you don't have to worry about some guy knocking on your door in the middle of your romantic evening.

If you drink alcohol, you are going to have a nice chilled white wine. I would make a suggestion but since I don't drink I will not take the chance of sounding foolish! If you don't drink buy a nice bottle of Non-alcoholic wine. (Get a soda for back up. I hate those things too!) Mainly, we just want the "appearance of a nice bottle of wine! (If you drink, use beer as a backup. Above all things, you want your date to be comfortable.) Now we need a bucket of ice for the wine. Assuming again that you own nothing, buy a small bucket from the dollar store. We will later drape it too with a pillowcase to hide the bucket. Finally, make a stop by the video store. Just walk right pass the Martial Arts and Horror flicks. Instead, look around the store until you find someone who is either wearing something your spouse owns or acting just like she does when you visit the video store together. Hopefully this person will also share her taste in movies. Swallow your shyness and ask this lady what she would prefer as a romantic comedy then get that video. If the store you are in is sold out, leave that store and go find the movie she suggested. Now all we need is some popcorn for the movie and a small radio with some "I need to hold you" music.

Back at home: Our table is draped in the center of the room. The couch is in a separate part of the room and the TV and VCR are in front of the couch. Any variation of this will do as long as the couch and the TV are in the background.

Cut the gift ribbons in one-yard lengths. Raking them between your thumb and the sharp side of the scissors or knife will make them curl. Use the scotch tape to hang them from the roof... not too low...not too high...just above your head. Yea, I know it's getting cheesy but remember this night is not for you. It's for her. You are making the room into one large surprise party! Next, blow up the balloons and scatter them all around everywhere! Place the video in the VCR and make sure it is rewound to kill any awkward moments. Cue the music! Place the candle! Ready the bucket of ice on the table! Step back and look at it all. It's looking good! Now we are ready to make the call.

It's time for the set up. Tell her that you and some friends are all going out to celebrate his new job and you have been asked to come and bring a date. Or maybe your grandmother or aunt has invited you over for dinner. Be nonchalant. This way, she will get dressed but not expect anything! Remember, our word for today is "surprise"! Try to time the pizza out so that it is good and hot! Hopefully you found a coupon. (Smile)

Candle—$1.00 Bucket—$1.00Popcorn—$2.00Movie—$3.00
Pizza—$10.00 Ribbon—$2.00Balloons—$2.00Drink —$5.00

The prices may vary but you get the idea. You have just spent $26 dollars on a night she will always remember. Take the extra four dollars and buy yourself a pat on the back. You deserve it. You are a good servant.

P.S. If your date complains all night about the cheap wine or the cheesy ribbons and balloons give her 5 points for every negative thing she says. When she accumulates over 10 points you will know she is crazy. A real lady would acknowledge all the trouble you have gone through to surprise her and will want to pat you on the head and make you feel like a good servant. Do not argue with the crazy person. She didn't get it and she will never appreciate what you did until you are doing it for someone else.

Loving on a shoestring budget is easy. All you need is imagination. I watch kids today playing with their expensive video games always wanting more. Each year there's a new game system that makes the one you took out a second mortgage for obsolete. I remember what it was like to build a bow and arrow from a tree limb and kite string. We formed our arrows from cattail sticks and fashioned arrowheads from bent bottle caps. Those weapons my brothers and I built were strong enough to pierce my father's tool shed. We were not poor. We were inventive. And yes, it got us plenty of good beatings but we had fun. Simple fun. That's all a budget is. Simple fun.

Budgets are relative. I've never been rich so I can't say what that budget would look like but I do know that women love simple things. Take your lady on a trip around the world if you can afford it, but don't forget to stop and smell the roses along the way.

When Tesha and I had no money we found so many simple things around town to do. Huntsville, Alabama is not Times Square but you would be surprised at how many wonderful hidden places it has. You have to learn how to plan. Sometimes I would scout around town for picnic places. Picnics are wonderful. If you have the money, I suggest that every couple invest in a quality picnic basket. You might want to write that down in the "notes" sections of this book, but until our ship comes in let's work with what we have.

Picnics are simpler than dinner so we will invest only $25 in this adventure.

First we take a trip to the closet. We are looking for the thickest quilt or blanket we can afford to spread on the ground. You want the blanket to be thick because the ground may be very hard. If we do not have a blanket to spare, you can usually pick one up at a thrift store for about $5.00.

Second, we scope out the picnic area looking for something relaxing. Don't be afraid to leave the city and take a ride through the country. You're almost certain to find that perfect spot in the country. If you choose this spot, make sure you get permission from the owner to have your picnic there. Getting arrested or shot for trespassing can ruin a picnic! If you can't leave the city, most city parks will do just fine. Pick a sight below the trees and check for bugs. Ants and mosquitoes can also ruin a romantic evening. Here is my first commercial plug. I have personally found "SkinSoSoft" by Avon to be perfect for warding off pests. It does not have the awful smell of a bug repellent and mosquitoes will not touch it! Add it to your picnic basket! Now hopefully Avon will read this book and send me a check. Also, beware of ducks! They are use to being fed and they carry their droppings wherever they go. If you plan on feeding the ducks do it last! Once you throw the first crumb, you own them or should I say, they own you.

Now that we have our blanket and romantic spot picked out, all we need is the food. We have quite a few choices here. We may have sandwiches and chips, a fresh fruit basket hand picked from your local grocer or our favorite; a nice home cooked meal. At any rate, I will allow a whopping $10 bucks for it! Splurge any way you want!

O.K. Whip out the calculator:

SkinSoSoft—$4 Food & Drink—$10 Blanket—$5

We have $6 dollars left. Can you think of anything we left out? How about some DESSERT!

Small assortment of Fruit -$3
Melted Chocolate Bar-$.50
Imagination—Priceless

Hey! We have $1.50 left! We can afford a little more fun. Quick! Back to the grocery store for as much fruit and chocolate you can afford. Then we go home! Don't forget to write your notes before moving on to the next section.

Notes

Notes

Fruit and Kisses

We will need a soft cloth to use as a blindfold. Melt the chocolate in one bowl and put the fresh mixed fruit in another. You can use the microwave to melt the chocolate bar but be very careful. Burnt chocolate does not help set the mood. Blindfold your mate. She will have to trust that you are not up to no-good. Once the blindfold is on you can uncross your fingers. One by one I first dip the fruit in the chocolate then feed my blindfolded love victim. When she thinks she knows how it all works I switch gears. First I touch the chocolate on her nose. Then I kiss it off. Using my deadly strawberry, I place more chocolate on her forehead, cheek & chin. Each time I softly kiss it off. Now that she knows she's been had, I put her in the driver's seat. The next time I dip my strawberry in the chocolate I place it in her hands and softly whisper into her ear. "Now you show me where". Then once again, I become the servant. See, I told you!! This servant life is pretty good. And it all started with a $25 dollar picnic.

My wife wanted me to leave that part out but I figured that if you bought the book I at least owe you one private game. At least I left out the part about…well, maybe we should just continue.

You can add some creativity to your picnic. What about a sunrise or sunset picnic? A small breakfast while watching the sunrise is incredibly romantic. Of course, the same goes for sunsets. If you are blessed to live by a beach this could be one of those moments you never forget. She certainly will not. And what did it cost you? I hate to ask that but remember we are on a budget. Be creative. Let the circumstances move you.

I have a friend named Teresa. Her husband promised to take her to the beach this summer but through no fault of his own, he was not able to make good on that promise. Instead of writing the whole adventure off, she decided to bring the beach home! She found some romantic beach scene videos and some ocean music and packed a beach lunch for an empty room upstairs!

The only thing she paid for was the beach balls and food. She got the video and music from her local library. As long as she returns them on time, they're free!

Notes

Notes

Get Out Of Debt

I'm sure we all can agree that living a debt free life will greatly improve your romantic life. Financial worries can ruin a perfect marriage. There are too many other factors in life and love to worry about. Let's get rid of this one. Easier said than done, right? Wrong! I have found two consumer advocates who make it pretty easy for us all. Since I'm not a financial advisor I will give you their web addresses so that you can try them for yourself. On these websites you will find show times and show archives.

Clark Howard—WWW.CLARKHOWARD.COM
Dave Ramsey—WWW.DAVERAMSEY.COM

When I'm in Atlanta, Ga. I tune into WSB 750AM and listen to Clark. When I'm in Huntsville, Al. I tune into WBHP 1230 AM and listen to Dave. Since these guys are nationwide your local A.M. radio station should carry one of them. If not, I would call that radio station and ask for one. After listening to one show your financial brain cells will be multiplied by ten. If you can't find enough people to help you protest outside these radio stations, you can simply listen to the show via Internet from both websites!

My brother-in-law and his family are currently taking Dave Ramsey's "Financial Peace University" course. He claims since taking the course he and his family have more than doubled their romance and family fun budgets. Their was so much more money once they learned how to budget properly. Plus, it's easier to enjoy yourself when you're out if you're not worrying about paying the bills.

These men sound so much alike they may be clones! Whatever the case, they have made my financial life easier to maintain which makes my love life more enjoyable. I'm sure you too will not be disappointed.

They say nothing in this world is free. Well, if this whole section was not a free commercial plug for Clark Howard and Dave Ramsey I don't know what it was! If you tune in or call these shows the advice they give will be free also. The simple truth is that even If I convinced a million of you to tune in I would still owe them.

Notes

Notes

The Vacation

You know it wasn't until I had a family of my own that I realized how poor my parents were. The reason I didn't know is because they provided everything we ever needed. How? I have no idea! I have four brothers and two sisters including a nephew that grew up with us like a brother. That's a total of ten people in our household. My parents took us on vacation every single year. I can't think of a single summer missed! When I asked my father how, he bellowed, "Family comes first!" This sounds pretty good but I figured I'd better get the details from my mother. Here is what she said, "I used an old purse that I kept in the back of my closet. After we cashed a check and before we went to sleep every night we would put something from our pockets into it and forget about it. Then you make a deadline for your vacation. When that date arrives, you will be surprised to see what you have saved! It was always enough!"

Now I know what you are thinking. "What about bills and emergencies?" Well my father answered that question a long time ago before I got married. He said, "Pay your bills on time. But don't forget you will always have them! Don't let bills dictate your life. If you are waiting to pay off all your bills before taking that cruise to Jamaica you will never go." Just getting away for the weekend has given us many memorable moments. One of those memorable moments is now a five-year-old little girl. So let me tell you how we got this five-year-old miracle. I call this one...

How to Kidnap a Loved One

At the time, I worked two jobs. I worked Monday through Friday with a cable company and Saturday through Sunday as a waiter. For those of you not counting, that means I literally worked every day! So if I could still find time to be romantic, I'm sure you can too. You have to make sacrifices. I'm not asking you to quit your job, but the simple truth is we work hard to make a better life for ourselves. So if you are not making a better life for the both of you, why are you working so hard? And at the end of the day can you look yourself in the mirror and honestly say she knows she comes first and she appreciates your hard work?

I skipped a weekend at the restaurant, sacrificing a weekend of pay, and planned a little get away for my wife. Tesha worked for a department store at the mall. I called her boss and explained to him what I had planned. He agreed not to schedule her for that particular weekend and not to tell her why.

Here is the plan. I heard through the grapevine that one of Tesha's favorite musical groups would be making an appearance in a very small city only three hours away. I didn't hesitate. I called the venue where the concert would be held. I could have used Ticketmaster but I wanted to talk to someone who could help me. I explained my idea to the attendant. I planned on kidnapping my wife and surprising her with the concert. She loved the idea. In fact, as I hoped, I paid for the best seats I could afford at that time and she promised to move us up if the chance presented itself. That's the human connection! By explaining my idea to her, she became part of the surprise. I now have two weeks left to get my plan right. That gives me time to shop around that city for a good deal on a hotel. Because remember, we are on a budget!

Don't be afraid to tell your story to anybody that can help you! Every time I told my idea to a hotel receptionist, the rooms got cheaper and cheaper!

I had many to choose from. I eventually secured a very nice suite for the price of a single. Supposedly, because it would be available and another group who would be staying there at the same time had secured all the single and double rooms, but I like to believe it was the "human connection". Now let's review for a moment. We have the tickets. We have the room. All we are missing now is THE WIFE.

Remember, the wife is going on with her week and has no idea what is being planned. The suspense is killing me. I borrowed a suitcase from her mother. I didn't use ours because I didn't want her to miss anything from the house. CLUE: Men, we can throw on a pair of dirty jeans and a sweaty T-shirt and go to church! This does not apply to women. You must, by law, buy her something NEW for a concert. It's written somewhere in the female manual. Just plan on it. Also, plan enough time for her to pick this item up from the mall. About two hours should do it. Now back to the story. Don't tell anyone local about the trip. Most people cannot keep a secret! I had to tell Mrs. Archie, Tesha's mom, but I swore her to secrecy. My mother-in-law has a serious poker face! She has never given up any of my secrets yet! In fact, she helped me make out a list of "woman-needs" to add to my suitcase.

Friday morning: Tesha and I got dressed for work as usual, I dropped her off and I went to work. We usually plan lunch together but today I am too busy for a lunch break, so she thinks. For lunch, I double back to our apartment and load the car. I over pack her things because I'm not quite sure what she will need. I go over my checklist. Car tuned and ready-check, Toothbrushes-check, Deodorant-check, Condoms—I told you about the five year old right? I can't think of everything!

That afternoon, I picked Tesha up as usual. She started to complain about her day. I listened quietly as I pulled onto the highway. She actually talked for thirty minutes before realizing we had left the city! "Where are we going?" she asked. "Hush!" I replied, "You have been kidnapped! If you want to help, you can navigate!" I tossed her a map showing her where I had circled Tupelo, Mississippi. Now, I knew what she was thinking. What in the world is in Tupelo, Mississippi?!?! I didn't answer any of her questions. I could see the excitement on her face and it made me feel good inside the way a good servant should feel. The trip was beautiful! We drove through the Natchez Trace stopping for everything that caught our eye and it didn't cost us a cent! When we pulled into the small sleepy town of Tupelo I purposely drove pass the coliseum. Her eyes where wandering around the town until she caught the sign outside the coliseum. "Tonight in concert—Boys II Men!" She literally screamed. I drove to the hotel. The receptionist was the same one I talked to on the phone. She said something to my wife that I didn't hear that made them both smile. I also noticed that the same thing happened when we picked up our tickets at the will call but listen to this.

The will call attendant had moved us from the back of the coliseum to about 10 feet from the stage! We were so close that every time a special effect exploded on stage, we could feel the heat from it! The human connection!

I will not tell you how much all of this cost but I will tell you that after all was said and done I had enough money left over to drive about one hour away from Tupelo into Memphis, Tennessee for lunch at BB Kings restaurant on Beale Street. Hey, Arkansas was just across the bridge so we went there too! In all, we had a wonderful time. I spent a little more than I planned but was it worth it? Well, her name is Khadijah LaShawn DeAnn Thompson, and we will never forget how she came about.

One day I plan on taking her on a cruise. Anywhere. Maybe if you tell your friend about this book and he tells his friend, I will be able to do it pretty soon! We'll just call it the "Send Tesha Around The World Fund".

But seriously, if you want to plan a really nice trip, visit a travel agent first. There are a million scams out there. Sometimes if it sounds too good to be true…well, you know the rest. Don't get burned. Make sure you know about all hidden cost before boarding the ship. If you are planning on visiting a different city, get as many brochures on that city as possible. That way you'll be sure not to miss anything. What was that my scoutmaster use to say all the time? Be prepared! Check out these two publications. "Travel Smart" & "The Educated Traveler".

Notes

Notes

Notes

Paying Attention

There is nothing more important in a relationship than paying attention. I have a friend who complains about his lady "asking" for too much! His word for her is "high maintenance". After reading a few pages of my rough draft he wanted me to agree with him and label her "crazy". After listening to his story we found that his lady only had one problem. He was not spoiling her correctly. Therefore he has no one to blame but himself. Plus, she never asked for anything unreasonable. At the time, my friend was working part-time while trying to finish college. She was not asking for a new mink coat. She would have easily gotten twenty points for that, putting her well above the "crazy" limit. The reason she had to "ask" for everything is because he was not paying attention to her clues.

Example: One day when Tesha and I were dating, I called her to see how she was doing. She was getting dressed for work and mentioned, jokingly, that she had holes in her socks but was going to wear them anyway. "Ding! Ding! Ding!" Did you hear it? She just gave me a clue that she needed a new pair of socks without asking for them! When she went to work I went to a ladies department store and bought my lady a couple pairs of socks. I stopped by a grocery store and picked up a bag of Jolly Ranchers (I found out she loved them from a previous clue!) and a couple of wild flowers from the flower department. Her mother let me into her bedroom where I placed the socks in the center of the bed. I opened the flowers and the bag of candy and placed them one by one strategically on the bed. Now when Tesha gets home late tonight she will flip on the light and immediately remember our earlier conversation about the socks! Of course she had to clean up this lovely mess before going to sleep but she never complained. She still remembers that day today and what did it cost me?

Jolly Rancher Candy—$1.50
Bouquet of Wild Flowers—$3.00
Socks—6/$5.00

Nine dollars and fifty cents and all I had to do was skip a night at the movies! My mother would have been proud of me and Tesha's mom started whispering in her ear, "He's the one!" All because I pay attention and pick up on clues. Tesha never asks for much but all that know us will admit that we are both pretty spoiled.

Try this exercise. As quick as you can, without much thought, jot down three things that your lady has never received or done in her past. Anything.

(1)_____

(2)_____

(3)_____

Now how can we turn these three answers into unforgettable surprises? Are your romantic juices flowing? We already know how she feels about them. It's not like we are walking into the store blind. Here's my list:

(1) Easy Bake Oven

(2) Travel (Anywhere!)

(3) To Own Her Own Business

There are plenty of things I could have named but I chose these three to make a point. Don't think about what would make a good gift or surprise. Just write. An "Easy Bake Oven" may sound childish but it's the first thing that popped into my mind.

I chose the "Easy Bake Oven" because, as a child, my wife once told me she circled it in a Sears Catalog for Christmas but never received it. To think of her ever wanting anything and not receiving it really bothers me. Although an "Easy Bake Oven" might be a child's toy, I think she would really love to receive one. Maybe she could live out that childhood dream while teaching our daughters to bake. And guess who gets the first cake out of the oven? That's right! Me! The good servant!

Traveling was second on my list because my wife often talks about places she'd like to go. Growing up, she never traveled much but always wanted to. She was so excited when I surprised her with an over night trip to Nashville for the weekend. Nashville is only one hour from where she grew up! Imagine how she's going to respond to that cruise to Jamaica!

Last on my list was her business. My wife is an extremely hard worker and she has a serious entrepreneurial spirit. My job as her husband is to help her any way I can to realize her dreams.

So here we have three very simple ideas for new surprises. We know all of these will make her happy because she has already told us so. All we had to do was pay attention!

Now if she berates you for buying her a child's toy or not borrowing above your means to pay for an expensive vacation, simply refer to the first two chapters of this book. She may be trying to tell you something that you have been over looking. She may be crazy!

Notes

Notes

Notes

The Little Things

It's amazing how big the little things in a relationship are. People usually don't get divorced over large problems. It's usually the little things that either you don't do or don't do correctly that seem to add up. When women get fed up they usually try to "coach" us into doing these little things. In male terms this is known as "nagging". Does your lady seem to "nag" you all the time? Have you taken a hard look at yourself? Unfortunately, most women have not figured out that this coaching process does not work and only makes them resemble the "crazy" lady. But for the sake of argument, let's assume it's our fault. Let's work on a little thing. Let me ask you. Do you know how to draw a bubble bath? Sure you do. You take a bath every day or at least you should. Let's build a bubble bath for two! All you have to do is remember two things. One—We are on a budget. And Two—This bath has nothing to do with getting clean!

Let's go back to the dollar store to pick up a few things. We are looking for tea candles. If you don't know what they are, they are very small candles wrapped in tin and usually come in a pack of six. Be careful not to let these burn too long. Although it has never happened to me, I have heard stories of them burning through the tin. You will also need "scented" candles. They are usually larger.

Make sure you don't forget the main ingredient…the bubble bath. Personally, my wife likes "Calgon". Wow, yet another commercial pitch. With every box you buy write "Calgon" a letter and tell them you only bought it because you read my book. Hopefully they will send me a few dollars to go into the "Send Tesha Around The World Fund". If you can't find "Calgon" try to find a bubble bath formula meant for kids. The bubbles are usually thicker and last longer. Although, bubble bath formulas made for adults usually contain water softener. "Calgon" seems to have the best of both worlds.

One quick stop by the flower department at your local grocer and we are ready. This time we are looking for roses! Pick three of the largest you can find. It would be better if they were fully bloomed because this time we are only interested in the petals.

At home, peel the petals off the roses and place them in a bucket. Strategically place your candles around the bath area. Find a way to pump in some romantic music but if you are using a small radio be extra careful not to place it in an area that will get wet like the floor. You don't want to put it in an area where it can fall into the tub either. You would be surprised at how unforgiving your lady will be if you electrocute her.

Run the shower for about a minute to get the room nice and steamy. As you run your bath water, add the bubble bath so that your bubbles will be huge! You can use any bubble bath or water softener you like but my wife personally likes Calgon. (I sure hope these commercial plugs pay off!) When your bath is complete with bubbles, feather your rose petals on top. Hopefully you will have enough to spill some over on the floor. Don't worry about the mess. It will look great! Now, go get the wife.

Hopefully you caught her off guard again. She thought you were taking a bath alone. There is Mrs. Thompson's word again, "Surprise!" Now turn off the lights and beneath the warm glow and scent of the candles and rose petals, you can take turns undressing each other!

Candles: Scented—2 x $1.00   Tea Candles—6 x $1.00
Roses—3 x $1.50   Calgon—$2.00

That's a total of $8.50. Plus, the only things you can't use again are the rose petals. What a bargain! You can enjoy this over and over again for the mere cost of the rose petals! Of course you don't want to do this every night, but you don't want to space them so far apart that she forgets either!

When your lady reminisces about the romantic times in your life together it should be like a buffet. And I promise, she will never think about the price!

Notes

Notes

Notes

A Picture is Worth a Thousand Bucks

I know the correct saying is "a picture is worth a thousand words," but we are on a budget. We need to stretch this picture business into a thousand bucks! All we need is two disposable cameras to do it!

Don't spend over ten bucks for the cameras. I have bought name brand and cheap cameras. The pictures look the same to me. As a matter of fact, some of the cheaper cameras actually took better pictures!

Tesha and I love sightseeing. We could make a day of visiting things around the city that we have never seen before. Why not take along a few disposable cameras? There's only one rule here. NO POSING! You both have separate cameras. Snap a quick pic of anything you desire without trying to control the other's camera. Women like to pose. Snap the picture before she can fix her hair but make sure you pay special attention to the warning at the end of this chapter!

Not only will this be fun but you will also have memories of this day for many days to come. Visit the park. Take a walk downtown. Visit a museum. The key to taking good pictures is taking a lot of them! You will be surprised at all the great shots you get of each other. If you have to break the rules and pose have a stranger take a shot of you both. Don't worry, even the most harden criminal can resist taking off with a disposable camera.

Now I don't want you to think that I know everything about women. There are some great mysteries out there. For example, have you ever noticed that women will spend five million dollars to make their hair perfect for one night but the most beautiful hairstyle every created is what? You got it…the wind blowing it all over the place. I bet you've heard this, "Roll the window up! It's blowing my hair!" Try this one. Women will also spend a small fortune on sexy lingerie but the sexiest thing ever created for women to wear to bed is…nothing covered with my button down shirt! Wow! It's like the Bermuda Triangle!

Warning: You should give your date some idea of what you are planning. Most women hate being surprised with a camera! Let her know you plan to take many pictures of her but you want her to dress casual. Trust me, it will be the dressiest casual you have ever seen but at least you gave her some kind of warning.

Notes

Notes

Just Because

If you really want to touch your love one's heart there is nothing better than a good "just because". It really doesn't matter how much you spend on a "just because". It catches her totally off guard. And when you can do that you have created a special moment in her heart forever!

Imagine it's lunchtime. She's walking out to her car. Her workload has doubled. Her boss is a fool and the day is only half over. She's thinking about grabbing some fast food and getting right back into the rat race. As she steps outside the sky breaks and it starts to rain cats and dogs!

She opens her car to find, neatly placed on her steering wheel, a beautiful rose and a letter. She opens it.

> Dear Tesha,
> I love you more than you will ever know
> I love you more than I could ever show
> I love you too much to ever let you go
> So please accept this simple rose
>
> I love you,
> Javier

I know it sounds "soupy" but remember it's not for you. It's for a lady having a horrible day. But now, thanks to your "soupy" letter, the sun cuts through the clouds. She's now able to put her foolish boss on 'ignore' and finish her work in record time because she can't wait to get home and show you how much that "soupy" letter meant to her!

Because we are on a budget I have to remind you that this little venture cost you less than three dollars. Even if you had to buy the pencil and a sheet of paper! Oh, and if you must, I give you full permission to use my "soupy" poem!

Here's your new assignment. List at least five more things you can do "just because".

1. _____

2. _____

3. _____

4. _____

5. _____

This is my list:

1. When you sit down tonight to have dinner, turn out the lights and add a candle.

2. Write her a letter about how much you truly love her. Here is the kicker: Mail it! Even if you are married! Especially if you are married!

3. Name a star after her! Dial International Star Registry at 1-800-282-3333. There's a small fee but it's worth it!

4) Buy her a book. Books are great gifts and they are still pretty cheap. If you are looking for a good book, look no farther than Oprah. Her book club always feature great gift books. Hopefully Oprah will read this and add my book to her list!

5) Take a walk in the park after work. If you have one in your city, take a nice carriage ride through the city. You will be surprised at how many people have never taken a carriage ride. You may be her first! If so, add twenty "Good Servant" points!

You should never let a week pass without at least one "just because". Also, these favors can be really inexpensive but you can also plan ahead for an expensive "just because". How do you think she would react if you flew her away for the weekend? It's not as expensive as you think. Especially if you don't have a set destination! Search the airlines for their best deals on weekend getaways and simply choose the one that fits your budget! I promise you'll be pleasantly surprised!

Delta.com will deliver weekend specials straight to your email inbox! Simply click on "special offers" and sign up! But don't stop there. Check out other airlines and compare! Many other airlines offer this same service. Southwest.com has a great weekend vacation package to Vegas that I'm drooling over now! These packages change cities but are always there. Just find the one that's right for you.

And when your loved one looks at you in amazement as she boards that flight and asks, "Why did you do this for me?" Simply say "just because!" and add fifty more "Good Servant" points.

O.K. I don't think you would do this but I have to say it anyway. Pretend that the flight was no big deal. I don't think I have to tell you that constantly repeating all the wonderful things you've done diminishes your "Good Servant" points. Even if she agrees that you are wonderful, she is secretly deducting points.

Notes

Notes

The Wishing Well

There was an old game show that would test a couple's knowledge of each other. The host would ask the same question to both the husband and wife then see if their answers matched. Most of the time the husband would be terribly wrong and would pay for not knowing something like where they first kissed with a swat over the head. I wonder how many divorces can be directly linked to that show?

I always thought that if I could get Tesha on one of those shows we could retire early off our winnings. Sometimes I feel like we've been together forever and that we know everything there is to know about each other. Of course this is not true. I think you can spend a lifetime together and not truly know everything there is to know about someone. So I invented a little machine to help you find some of her hidden wants and desires. It's called a Wishing Well.

What you will need.

1. An old shoe box
2. Some nice wrapping paper with no holiday themes
3. Scissors
4. Ink pen and marker (I like Sharpie)
5. Small writing pad

You should be able to find all of these things at a dollar store for less than five dollars or you may even have most of these items around the house.

Wrap the box in the wrapping paper and cut a hole in the top. Write on the outside of the box "Wishing Well" and place the ink pen and pad beside the box. Guess what? You are finished! That's it.

When you want to use the box write your wish on the small sheet of paper. Fold the wish and write her/his name on it. Periodically, check the box for notes addressed to you.

Most people have a hard time asking for things. Most people hate when someone asks them for things. This way she can let you know some of her wishes without having to be so forward. When you need quick romantic surprises you can go to your wishing well.

It's important that she writes down as many wishes as possible. Don't worry about filling up the box. Try. If you allow her to only write one or two wishes you will find her waiting for you to respond to those wishes in a timely manner. Make sure you explain that these are wishes and not a box of demands or expectations. Also, don't forget to add your wishes. I may need a separate box!

Tesha and I also have a prayer box. We write them down together and place them in a box just like the wishing well. At the end of the year we sit down and open them just to see how good God has been to our family. You know what? Most of the problems that were so big at the beginning of the year are so easily forgotten by the end of the year. I couldn't possibly know the religion of all my readers but I think the saying "a family that prays together stays together" is universal.

Notes

Notes

Around The Kitchen

My wife believes that a man in the kitchen is very sexy. Well, honestly, she prefers I stay out of the kitchen but that she believes that was all I needed to know. Fortunately for me Mrs. Thompson gave me the basics of cooking. Basically, if something wasn't cooking by the time she got home from work, there was hell to pay. She made sure that all five of her boys plus a nephew knew their way around the kitchen. My brother Donald and my sister Peaches can take flour and water and make Christmas Dinner! I've never been that good but I do follow directions well. Give me a good cookbook and BAM! I'm Emeril Lagasse!

Now I know women like surprises but sometimes making things together can be really nice. This is a stress free dinner. First we make it together then we eat it together. It's a family project. This is where we find out if we can work together. There are only two rules for this night.

Rule (1)
She chooses the menu but it must be something she has never had before.

Rule (2)
Inside the kitchen, you are the chef. She is the lowly assistant. Remind her that you only invited her into your world-renowned kitchen because you thought she would like to see how a masterpiece is created! Right?! Plus it is impossible to sauté fresh onions properly while holding a fire extinguisher.

Now, let's go find a cookbook. They are everywhere. You can find a good cookbook from the thrift store or the library. Some grocery stores even have little machines that will print out a nice recipe for you. There are countless magazines and millions of Internet sites. I suggest you go to a bookstore and search the bargain table. I found a very expensive cooking "encyclopedia" which once sold for $65 for only $10. I quickly pushed over the elderly lady who saw it first and claimed my prize! This cookbook was so nice that I don't even have it anymore! I guess what comes around goes around but the fact still remains that I found a great book for a great bargain and you can too!

After explaining the rules, give her a pen and paper and allow her to put together a nice menu for a nice Saturday night dinner. She can take as long as she wants but when she hands over the menu, all bets are final!

O.K. here is the tricky part. Of course when she picked this menu she did not have our budget in mind. Don't mention it. Don't be "crazy" and kill the mood. Keep your wallet in the back of your mind. Think man!! We need coupons!! So where do you find good coupons?

(1) Sunday paper   (2) Grocery store
(3) In the mail   (4) Internet

In the back of this book you will find a coupon source guide. It's just a small list of some of my favorite places to find coupons with room to add your own. There is nothing wrong with clipping and saving coupons. Some of my best ideas for a romantic night have come from first finding the appropriate coupon! Just remember two things. Don't turn flips in the isle every time you find a product for which you have a coupon and having a coupon does not mean it's the best product for the meal! Have fun in the grocery store. This is pre-date foreplay. It should be fun choosing the ingredients together. This could be a great time to learn how to budget together. Set a budget together and try to stay true to it. If you splurge, let it be for important items that you can't do without. Important things like strawberries and whip cream! Tesha can't live without them so therefore they become necessities unarguable.

Your date will probably never mention the coupons but if she makes a huge deal out of it and cancels the dinner...well...you know. She's probably "crazy". Trust me, if your date is crazy, you'll want to know before dessert!

Notes

Notes

The Massage and The Message

Sometimes, as a man, it's hard to say how you truly feel. You want to say "I love you" but it just doesn't sound right. You wonder if she knows how much she means to you. You can't write it and Lord knows you can't sing it.

I promise, this is something your lady will never forget. Here are the key ingredients:

(1) Bottle of Johnson & Johnson's Baby Oil
(2) Radio with CD and cassette player
(3) New blank cassette tape.
(4) Five of the greatest love songs ever written!

First, I search through my CD collection for my best love songs. Then I search my brother's collection. My sister Francesca might have a few that I need and she lives really close to my friend Jonathan who just happens to have a nice collection of music himself. I might even find what I'm looking for at the public library.

My wife loves Kenny "BabyFace" Edmonds. On his album "For the cool in you" he has a song that I can use to let my wife know that "I believe that a woman is the most precious thing on earth. And I'll do anything. I do mean anything. I don't won't my baby to hurt for a thing." Yea, that's exactly what I was going to say. Surely Kenny had me in mind when he wrote that. Now how can I sneak that Luther Vandross album away from my brother Donald? I know Luther would want to put his two cents in on this tape I'm making.

As you choose songs, you will be forced to realize what these songs mean to your relationship. These artists are saying all those things that were just on the tip of your tongue, aren't they? Good! Now pick up some pen and paper and write it down! No matter how stupid it sounds. Write it! Before every song we record on this tape we are going to talk about why we chose it and what we want her to think about while she listens to it. But don't write a speech. Just jot down notes! After all, this is coming from your heart, not my book!

Let's get started. Place the tape in the radio and press record. Count to five in your head then start a small introduction followed by the first song. When that song ends, introduce the next song. Don't be afraid to tell her how you really feel. If you mess up rewind and try it again but don't rewind just to hear yourself talk because trust me—you "will" sound dumb! But hey, this tape is not for you. It's for someone who will never forget how incredibly thoughtful and sexy your unrehearsed cracking voice sounded. Each song now takes on a different meaning to her when she hears it on the radio. As she hums the melody in public or at work people will stare at her and wonder what she's smiling about. So stop rewinding the tape and get it finished! There's more.

Now that we have the tape we need to learn how to give a good massage. You might take a trip to the library to read about technique but keep in mind, people are different. When you are giving the massage pay attention. She will let you know what feels good and what does not. She'll even tell you how much pressure to use. Resolve in your mind that no matter how much you want to, you will not stop! A massage is not quick. It's slow and soothing. Start with the toes and work your way up. Pay special attention to tight muscles being careful not to hurt her. Pay close attention to those places that give her pleasure. Trust me, you will both know when you touch them. In the back of your mind you have to remember that this is not just a massage. It's a "sensuous" massage. With every caress your fingers are telling her "I adore you!"

Now how do we get this started? My favorite is the shower. When she comes home tell her that you have something to tell her but it's important that she only listens. When she agrees prepare the shower. I don't know about your lady but Tesha likes the bathroom steamy so I let it run for a minute.

Now listen close guys because I learned this one from my daddy. When the shower is ready I invite my lady. As I slowly undress her I shower her with small kisses. Nothing too wild. (Yet!) Just little hints to let her know that I'm up to something special. Once you are both in the shower make sure that you are still in control. The purpose of this shower is not to get clean! If there is any washing going on, I will be doing it! I start with her feet. Like the servant I am, I wash them softly and humbly. The key words here guys are "soft" and "humble". And remember, no talking! Strictly forbidden! Let her imagine what's next.

When you are done leave her alone in the shower to wash the spots you missed but didn't really care about. Ask her not to leave the shower, as you will be back for her. This is very important because of two reasons.

(1) You need time to set up the radio.
(2) You don't want her to put on any clothing before you get back!

I place the radio as close to the bed as possible so that she can hear me clearly on the tape. I also place the baby oil next to the bed out of sight and slip into something comfortable before returning to the shower. She probably noticed that I removed "all" drying towels from the bathroom prior to the shower. She has no choice but to wait for me soaking wet.

Although I like her that way, I dry her off and lead her to the bedroom with small steps and little kisses. She thinks she knows what comes next but she is so wrong. As she relaxes on the bed I reveal the oil and start the tape. As she listens I encourage her to close her eyes and try to relax.

Don't get lost in the moment! This is her moment! Concentrate on what you are doing. Don't massage the places that feel good to you. Try to follow her lead.

The tape will be new for us but the shower and massage is not. The baby oil is a personal choice. We both like the way it glides and for some reason we have never found a massage oil that we like. I usually start with her toes and she's sleeping like a baby before I can reach her navel. I cover her with a light blanket and leave her there. Since having kids, I have learned to close and lock the door. You only have to hear "Why is mommy naked?" once to remember that!

Hey, I almost forgot. We are still on a budget. So what did this day cost us?

$2 Cassette Tape
$2 Johnson & Johnson baby oil

Four dollars! Now before you read this book, how many of you were thinking, "Hey, I've got five bucks! I think I will give my wife a night she will never forget and buy myself a Coke with the change!"

I checked out the massage book from the library. I borrowed the CD's because "stole" is such an ugly word. Besides, I think the Luther Vandross CD was really mine anyway!

Notes

Notes

Taking Care Of Mothers

It is my personal belief that there is no possible way to love another woman on this earth if that love does not originate between a man and his mother. It's not something you rehearse or plan. By loving me, my mother taught me how to love my wife. She also taught me that nothing comes between a man and his wife. Not even mothers. I hope that makes sense to you because I have a friend that's going through a terrible divorce right now because, in my opinion, his mother failed to cut the umbilical cord!

Tesha's mother, Mrs. Archie, is also very close to my heart. Not just because she gave birth to the most wonderful woman in the world, but because she too has always been there for me. One summer, when I was in college and Tesha and I were only dating, Mrs. Archie allowed me to stay with her so that I would not loose the job that was subsidizing my tuition. I will always be in debt to her for that because I can't say that I would do the same for my daughter's boyfriend. (If I ever allow my daughter to have a boyfriend!) There are plenty of stories about how my mother-in-law has come to our rescue but that one will always be in my heart.

Now I know that I have been blessed when it comes to mothers and mother in laws. I know that some of you are not as fortunate to have such good working relationships. Well, here's my advice. Fix it! Make it your responsibility. Love and respect her for who she is alone. Yea, even if she's crazy. If you love her daughter and that daughter has become everything in your life, as she should be, then you owe her mother everything! Think of it this way. If you had to purchase your wife from her, what would it cost? What is your lady worth? Tesha would still be on Lay-A-Way!

Seriously, every time I do something nice for Tesha's mother it's as if I did it double for her. That's true for every woman I know. Try it. Tomorrow, plan something very simple to honor the mother of the woman you love. A simple bouquet of flowers, candy or dinner! Let her know how much you appreciate her just for having the lady you love. Notice I said "tomorrow". Today, stop what you are doing and call your own mother! What were you waiting for, Mother's Day?

And today only, forget the budget. You owe these ladies big!

Notes

Knights and Heroes

Having a budget keeps us focused on our goals. It's no wonder that most divorces are caused by finances. A good man will actually destroy himself financially to make his lady happy. Ironically, a good woman is not overly concerned with his finances.

I don't want you to think that this book condones "cheapness". As your finances grow, so should your budget. I have plans for my wife that I can't afford right now but that does not stop me from dreaming.

Make plans for your future. Real plans. Your love should grow and evolve. I know a couple that has been together for five years. Yet, he still would rather spend the day with his friends and often forgets important dates and times. Often she has no idea where he is or when he will return. Is this love? Is this relationship growing, stagnant, or diminishing? Can it be saved? I don't know and even if I did, I would never give that kind of advice. I do know that he is taking her for granted and soon he may find someone else paying more attention to her.

Every woman has the potential to be a good woman. Every man has the potential to be a good man. Yes, even "crazy" people. My marriage works because I am genuinely concerned about my wife's happiness. There's a whole world out there trying to destroy her so it's me against the world. I'm her hero. I'm her knight. I still spend time with my friends but I would never choose them over my wife. Why would you plan a lifetime with anyone less?

I budget because I don't have "dream" money at this point in my life but I don't ever want her to doubt my love for her so I give her serious quality time. With every budgeted event I plan, she knows I'm planning and dreaming about her.

Notes

In Conclusion:
What Women Really Want

So what do women really want? For this answer I decided to go right to the source. I invited some of my married and dating friends to a "Romance Forum". Basically, I would hand out questionnaires to the women and aprons to the men as they arrived for the forum. The questionnaires would pick the women's brains about romance and dating issues. And for their participation, we men would treat them like queens all night. I really have wonderful friends. Friends like Alisha Green who didn't mind hosting my Romance Forum and inviting some of her friends. All I had to do was compose a few good questions, provide a babysitter and find something for the men to do while their wives filled them out. The men had only two jobs. Do whatever your lady requested while preparing dinner. Well, let me tell you this. When I passed the idea pass the wives, not one, I repeat, not one thought her husband would approve. So I told this surprising fact to the men and guess what? Not one man disagreed with my plan. In fact, two of my best friends, Paco and Jonathan became quite offended that their wives did not believe that they would make perfect servants! At that point we all decided to not only be perfect servants but also border line slaves! We would rub feet; massage backs and hand feed grapes all night if we had to! That will teach them! They'll be sorry!

My wife and Alisha helped me come up with the questions and they were pretty good. For example: Ask your lady this question. Don't forget that her answer is describing her love life with you!

What is the difference between what you thought romance would be and what it turned out to be in your adult relationships?

What I have found is that most women thought romance would be made of the kind of stuff that's found between the pages of their favorite fairy tale. But then we men came along dragging reality behind us and

107

ruined it. So did they turn their backs on us and wait for the next knight in shining armor? No, they SETTLED! That's right. They took us in knowing that we didn't have a romantic bone in our bodies.

Why does this have to be? Why is it so hard for us to be romantic? Why do we allow the women of our dreams to give up on ever finding that storybook romance?

Maybe you're saying to yourself, "Sometimes I'm romantic! I buy nice gifts on her birthday! We do something fun every Valentine's Day! I never forget important dates!" Hopefully you know me well enough by now to know that I don't give points for THINGS YOU ARE SUPPOSE TO DO!

Here are some more interesting questions that where on the questionnaire. Ask them in this order.

1) What is your definition of a thoughtful man?
2) What is your definition of a romantic man?
3) Which would you rather have?

First, we made the women separate the two definitions so that we could get a purer definition of what a romantic man is. What percentage do you think chose a thoughtful man over a romantic man? How about 99%! I wasn't sure what this meant. I thought romance would win hands down. The reasons were all different but I couldn't help but wonder if all these women had "settled".

The Romance Forum was a great success. I got all the answers I was looking for and after we served the women dinner and played a few games, everyone left smiling! Maybe that's because Paco saved our butts in the kitchen! The boy can burn! No cookbook needed! Of course we quickly served everything he cooked and stole all the credit. It's a dog eat dog world! Besides, Paco was the only Yankee in the house! Can't let too many people know he out did us southern folks! It goes against nature for anybody to know how to cook like that but not know what grits are!

So what do good women want? They want good men. They want someone who can be faithful, thoughtful and sincere while restoring their faith that fairy tales do come true. We can do that can't we? Good men aren't hard to find.

I remember when Tesha and I were dating I would ride up on my red VW Scirrocco and steal her away. I would slay her dragons and return her to her castle unharmed. O.K. so maybe I'm waxing poetically but you get the point. Most women have dreams of finding that man who is both thoughtful and romantic. That's what makes us good men. They don't want us to be perfect. Just every now and then, think of something romantic to do on your own without her coaching you. Be spontaneous. Be surprising! Every man can do that. If you are not trying to help her obtain her dreams and goals you are neglecting her. She deserves her storybook ending. And if you don't love her enough to do this simple thing, let her go so she can find a good man that will. You may be too "crazy" to love a good woman.

Notes

Notes

Testimonies From The Other Side
Of The Bed

How many of you are out there wondering if this guy is for real? Well, let me, the wife, be the first to relieve you of doubt. Do know that my husband is a good man. I will never forget when he proposed to marry me. It wasn't very formal and he didn't have a ring. We were just sitting and talking in our low rent, barely furnished apartment. We were reading because we didn't have a television or telephone. Suddenly, out of nowhere, he asked me to marry him. With no hesitation I said yes. I didn't say yes hoping for a richer future. I said yes because I knew he was the man I wanted to spend the rest of my life with. When people ask me how I knew he was the one, I simply say I had no doubts or reservations. Before he asked me I felt complete (let's not get mushy) with him. Javier has a way of loving you that makes you feel as if you are the queen of the world and if I just whisper my desires, he will provide.

Anyway moving on…let me elaborate on some of the girl talk we had at the Romance Forum 2000. May I do that, ladies? And yes, I said ladies because I know we read more than men. To my husband's disappointment, women will probably give this book to men. One of the topics were "Your man: Is he thoughtful or romantic?" Most said their man was thoughtful and that is what they would rather have. Well, Javier is a romantic and that is what I rather have. I never know what is going to happen next. It may be a trip or a night out on the town. Now don't get me wrong. I really appreciate the thoughtful part of him but I have grown to expect that part of him because of who he is.

Fact, since children there has not been much time for romance.

Fact, children did not curve my appetite for romance.

When you have three beautiful crumb snatching, ankle-biting rug rats, a thoughtful man is the best thing to have around. Someone to give them a bath when he comes home, take them out on "ER" night, or take over so I can sleep late on the weekend. That is a thoughtful man to me. Don't bring me flowers just take the kids!

So I'll shout it from the mountaintops, "I have a good man!" He has unconditionally loved me, always supported me and nonforcingly led me. Oh, how I love that man of mine!

Note that he is the head of our household but he knows that the head does not exist without the backbone and that's me. He is chauvinistic but not as much as he would have you believe. He has no problem tying on the apron and running the vacuum.

Ladies, don't be labeled the crazy one in your relationship. Men are not the greatest showers of affection. So when your man attempts to be romantic, show him you appreciate it. If you do this and he sees how much you enjoy it, and he's not the crazy one in the relationship, then he will continue to attempt to make you happy. Hopefully over time, he will become better at it! Yes, I know its ego stroking but what's wrong with making your man feel like he's the king of the world? He's your king isn't he?

For example, my brother, bless his heart, is not the most affectionate, or tactful in that case, man in the world. But having been told by his lady that she enjoys hugs and kisses and cuddling, he has improved. He's not a wealthy man by far, but he wanted to show her a sincere apology for one of his foul ups. Not having enough money for a bouquet of roses, he made her a bouquet of her favorite snack cakes. He purchased a nice, low priced, craft like vase, a couple sheets of white tissue paper, a pack of kabob skewers, and a box of the Little Debbie snack cakes. He placed the cakes, still in the wrapper (You wouldn't give her dead roses, don't give her stale cakes), on the point of each skewer. He then neatly wrapped the bundle in the tissue paper and placed it in the vase. Now when you present this you have to give a real apology with it and believe me for what he did he really had to apologize.

That was just another example of that whole budget and love thing. You don't have to go into debt to prove your love. You just have to make sure that person isn't...you know...crazy.

Personally, I like receiving gifts that took a little work. Anyone can buy a gift but only the most thoughtful, romantic and creative men can build one.

Notes

Notes

Notes

Notes

Notes

"THE MERE IMPARTING OF INFORMATION IS NOT EDU-CATION. ABOVE ALL THINGS, THE EFFORT MUST RESULT IN MAKING A MAN THINK AND DO FOR HIMSELF."

—CARTER G. WOODSON

Coupon Source Guide

1) Newspapers—Every city in America has a really nice Sunday Sales Section just add scissors.

2) Internet—A few of my favorites are Hotcoupons.com, Coolsavings.com, Coupons.com, CouponPages.com & About.com

3) Grocery Stores—Grocery Stores usually keep stacks of their current sales papers in the front of the store. If you're looking for a certain brand, you can usually find them in the aisle.

4) Check your receipts. Many stores have started printing their receipts on coupons.

5) Mailers—You know those letters addressed to "Current Resident"? Stop throwing them away.

Coupon Source Guide

1) _____
2) _____
3) _____
4) _____
5) _____
6) _____
7) _____
8) _____
9) _____
10) _____
11) _____
12) _____
13) _____
14) _____
15) _____
16) _____
17) _____
18) _____
19) _____
20) _____
21) _____
22) _____
23) _____
24) _____
25) _____
26) _____
27) _____
28) _____
29) _____
30) _____

Helpful Internet Sites

1) Just a few to get you started like Creativedates.com, PCKPublications.com, lovingyou.com, getromantic.com, theromantic.com, hopelessromantic.com & romance-tips.com.

2) _____

3) _____

4) _____

5) _____

6) _____

7) _____

8) _____

9) _____

10) _____

11) _____

12) _____

13) _____

14) _____

Important Dates and Times

1) _____

2) _____

3) _____

4) _____

5) _____

6) _____

7) _____

8) _____

9) _____

10) _____

11) _____

12) _____

13) _____

14) _____

15) _____

16) _____

17) _____

About the Author

As I started to list my personal accomplishments it suddenly struck me. Who cares? The only worthwhile accomplishment I have that should concern you is that my wife and kids think I'm superman. So here's my idea. Let's pretend you wrote this book. You also graduated from the Javier School of Love and have more degrees than a thermometer!

0-595-21087-2

www.ingramcontent.com/pod-product-compliance
Lightning Source LLC
Chambersburg PA
CBHW061305280526
45784CB00002B/901